IMAGES
of America

CONNECTICUT STATE POLICE

This is a view of 100 Washington Street in Hartford. The former residence of the Gov. Morgan Bulkeley, it was headquarters from approximately 1910 to 1939. Bulkeley was also the president of the National Baseball League. When the decision was made to knock down the Bulkeley Mansion, the Connecticut State Police Department relocated its headquarters into the barn and carriage house on the property. Cars and motorcycles were on the first floor, and the loft was converted to office space. (Author's collection.)

On the Cover: State policemen are about to head out on patrol around 1940 from Main Street in Stafford Springs, Connecticut. Stafford Springs was the former location of Station C, then the Troop C Barracks. (Author's collection.)

IMAGES
of America

CONNECTICUT STATE POLICE

Jerry Longo

ARCADIA
PUBLISHING

ISBN 978-1-4671-2021-0

Published by Arcadia Publishing
Charleston, South Carolina

Printed in the United States of America

Library of Congress Control Number: 2013932794

For all general information, please contact Arcadia Publishing:
Telephone 843-853-2070
Fax 843-853-0044
E-mail sales@arcadiapublishing.com
For customer service and orders:
Toll-Free 1-888-313-2665

Visit us on the Internet at www.arcadiapublishing.com

To the men and women of the Connecticut State Police Department, who have all sworn an oath to perish rather than swerve from their path of duty

Contents

Acknowledgments

Connecticut State Police Alumni Board members and associates provided much needed support, with special mention going to those troopers and troopers' families who parted with their precious photographs. Much of the author's gratitude goes to the department of emergency services and public protection for its kind attention to this project.

I appreciate the tolerance of my wife, Veronica, in allowing me to fill the office at home during this endeavor with seemingly endless boxes of photographs. A salute goes out to retired Connecticut State Police lieutenant Edward Steele, who turned 100 in 2013, and was a reliable source of identification and information for the book.

All of the photographs were collected personally or were accessed from the Connecticut State Police Academy Alumni Museum and Educational Center. Assistance was provided by Joseph "Photo Joe" Weronik and retired sergeant Ken Barton, the alumni newsletter's editor.

INTRODUCTION

The latter half of the 19th century in Connecticut was marred by the expansion of intoxicating liquors into the cities, towns, and boroughs of this small but influential state.

Most of Connecticut's citizens did not want liquor everywhere. They did not want it sold on Sundays or illegally at any time. The problem was both one of supply and demand along with a corruptible law enforcement community. Because many of the law enforcement agents at the time were operating with disregard for these violations or protected the violators, the public clamored for the end of liquor violators and violations of Sunday closing laws.

In June 1871, a bill was written to establish a state police department. This bill failed due partly to the argument that sheriffs and constables would lose revenue from serving subpoenas and other court and civil functions. Ironically, only two states, Rhode Island and Connecticut, would later fail to ratify the Eighteenth Amendment to the Constitution, which established Prohibition.

The temperance movements and citizens thought the answer was the establishment of an organization known as the Law and Order League, which started in 1884. This group was not very successful and would be reborn in 1892 as the Citizens Law and Order League. One unique thing about this group was that women were encouraged to join. Known as Spotters, its agents carried weapons, prepared cases, and went to court.

In 1895, the group would revert back to its original name, having had some success, and the governor of the state would appoint members on the state payroll to its list of agents reporting back to him. The league's premise was simple—to report on and arrest violators abusing existing laws using agents of the organization who would prepare cases and have local constables or sheriffs make the arrests. At the time, its secretary was the president of Yale, Noah Porter, and it had many other prominent citizens on its rosters.

Then, in 1899, at the state capitol, Rep. Joseph Barbour presented a bill to create the state police department and to put electric lights in the building. The lights were installed in the capitol, but the police bill was defeated. Those who did not want to see the state have an organized police department would fight for another eight years.

A new bill establishing a state police department in 1903 called for five commissioners whose duties included selecting a superintendent, assistant superintendent, and from five to ten policemen. Their goal was put forth simply as follows: enforce laws pertaining to liquor violations, prevent crime, preserve the peace, and secure the detection, arrest, and conviction of offenders.

The legislature set the pay for the new officers at $3 per day. They also were allotted $138 in expenses. The department's total operating expenses were pegged at $13,737.59 for its year of inception.

In May 1903, House Bill 247 was sponsored by Samuel Thrasher of the Law and Order League but was introduced by Harry Goslee, the representative from Glastonbury. Gov. Abiram Chamberlain signed the bill on May 27, 1903.

The Connecticut State Police Department Commission's founding members were Frank T. Brown of Norwich (lawyer), Yale Law graduate Henry English of New Haven (son of the late governor James E. English), James Huntington of Woodbury (state's attorney and judge of probate), John H. Perry of Southport (judge and speaker of the Connecticut House of Representatives), and Marcus H. Holcomb of Southington (judge and treasurer of Hartford County). These first five members served under this established bipartisan commission. There were 11 candidates for superintendent. The man selected was Thomas F. Egan, a deputy sheriff of Southington. Of the four applicants for assistant superintendent, Arthur L. Story of Norwich was selected.

The first five sworn members of the new state police department were Merrill S. Louks of Ashford (former Law and Order League detective), William G. Clark of Bethel (former constable), Frank

C. Barnes of Plymouth (former constable), John S. Flynn of Wethersfield (former prison guard), and William O'Brien of New Haven (former constable).

For many months and until those men were hired, the only active officers were the superintendent and the assistant superintendent. Egan made the first arrest, of saloon owner John Fowler, when he noticed Fowler open on Sunday. Egan, who was on the way to church with his family, told the bar owner he would be arrested the next day.

Egan successfully investigated a burglary of a saloon. On October 18, 1903, Egan, Story, and a sheriff raided a house of ill repute. All of the accused received $7 fines.

The very next day, October 19, the first of the five officers was hired. According to reports filed to the state police commission, William O'Brien was the first officer hired. This was due to his having been the first to get bonded, which was a requirement of the commission.

At the end of 1903, Egan files a report to the commissioners declaring the year had 35 arrests and 34 convictions. Egan hired Clara Ware of Middletown to run the day-to-day business in the office; her salary was pegged at $600 per year; her father was a prison guard at the Wethersfield Prison and a prominent businessman.

With the addition of the first five officers, the responsibilities shifted from Egan's shoulders to theirs. They sometimes had to travel for days by trolley, train, or even rented horses to the sites of criminal offenses; it proved to be an extremely difficult lifestyle.

This new department grew quickly in size from 5 officers in 1903 to 50 in 1921. During this growth in personnel, many other responsibilities were added.

During the wars, especially World War II, there was an expansion of responsibilities that has been unmatched since. The defense council was replaced with the war council and was headed up by state police commissioner Edward Hickey. That council had a budget of just a little less than $3,000,000 per year. One of the first actions taken by the council was to make all of the security personnel at defense plants special state police. After these personnel were added along with 1,200 auxiliary troopers, the state police had approximately 5,000 people on its payroll or under its charge.

During the early phases of the Cold War, state police, in one example of home defense, handed out more than 70,000 pamphlets on how to survive an atomic bomb attack. These 299 men and women also carried Geiger counters in their vehicles. One part of the home defense option saw troopers attending the christening of the first nuclear submarine, *Nautilus*, at New London, Connecticut. These actions of civil defense would carry on into the 1970s.

Many large sections of the state police department's actions and history, especially from 1903 to approximately 1920, were lost or destroyed. In many cases, the only surviving records were those found in the executive branch of government because of the oversight and involvement of the five original and subsequent commissioners.

One

The Beginning 1903–1919

The state police department's office opened at the capitol in 1903. Clara Ware and Bertha Sharpe oversaw the entire budget, with expenses for each officer set at $138 per year.

The next year, 54 men were arrested for violating liquor laws. In the papers, the arresting officers are referred to as gumshoe men. Also in 1904, Officer Merrill Louks was the first officer shot in the line of duty, and the man who shot him, John Whipple, would take his own life.

In 1905, the state police took on the duty of fire marshal, and also that year, a man named Goodwin was likely the first arrested for speeding in Connecticut. A 1905 bill was presented to abolish the department; however, the solving of a murder case by means of interviewing a child garnered so much respect for the department that the bill was overturned.

In 1906, a reporter photographed a state police officer for the first time, and troopers took over the registration of movie houses. At that time, officers were making $18 per week. In 1908, during a raid above a funeral home, some of those arrested were hiding in caskets.

In 1909, burglar Alice Skinner was arrested, and she told future superintendent Robert Hurley that she would have blown his head off if she had been given the chance. Around that time, state police were told to control pawnbrokers.

In 1911, the superintendent purchased the first department motorcycle, and the 1911 Henderson Excelsior was to be operated by Officer Rowe Wheeler. The responsibilities of weights and measures were added to the duties of officers.

The state police officers quelled a 1912 riot at the Russell Manufacturing Company, and the years 1913 and 1914 saw the growth of arson cases and motor vehicle thefts. During this period, the state police became wildlife officers.

In 1916, Amy Archer-Gilligan was arrested and tried; she killed tenants of her nursing home. Her serial killings would become a Broadway play titled *Arsenic and Old Lace*, which was later made into a movie.

World War I saw the state police department hire women to act as matrons, while dozens of spies were investigated and arrested by federal and state officers.

This photograph shows officers and vehicles lined up for inspection. Many officers from this time period did not fulfill their entire length of duty due to the extreme working conditions and were gone after just months or, at best, a couple of years. Since they worked around the clock for 30 days at a clip with one day off per month, being married when applying was not encouraged. The photograph was discovered beneath another photograph, having been used as filling behind that picture of lesser importance.

This image was found in a file drawer in an abandoned facility; the location and the officer pictured are both unidentified. Though a valuable tool in the law enforcement arsenal, the motorcycle has proven to be the most costly device for the state police, accounting for many of its fatalities.

Beginning in 1911, motorcycles were the main transportation choice during good weather. That was the year the commissioner purchased the first motorcycle, a Henderson. Hendersons would be the go-to vehicle for the department and were similar to those at Station D in Danielson, Connecticut, the location of this photograph. Station D was known for its distinctive garage.

At first, state police stations, substations, and barracks were spread out along the state's borders to provide maximum protection against the flow of liquor, drugs, and ladies of ill fame. They were also placed at the highest concentration points for vehicular traffic, such as this location in Beacon Falls, Connecticut.

The first members of the state police would work 30 days at a time out of barracks and would only travel home during that period if given authorization. At an average of $3 to $4 per day, there was not much left over for a family or social life, and so married applicants were strongly advised to think twice before joining. Pictured are officers in Troop B.

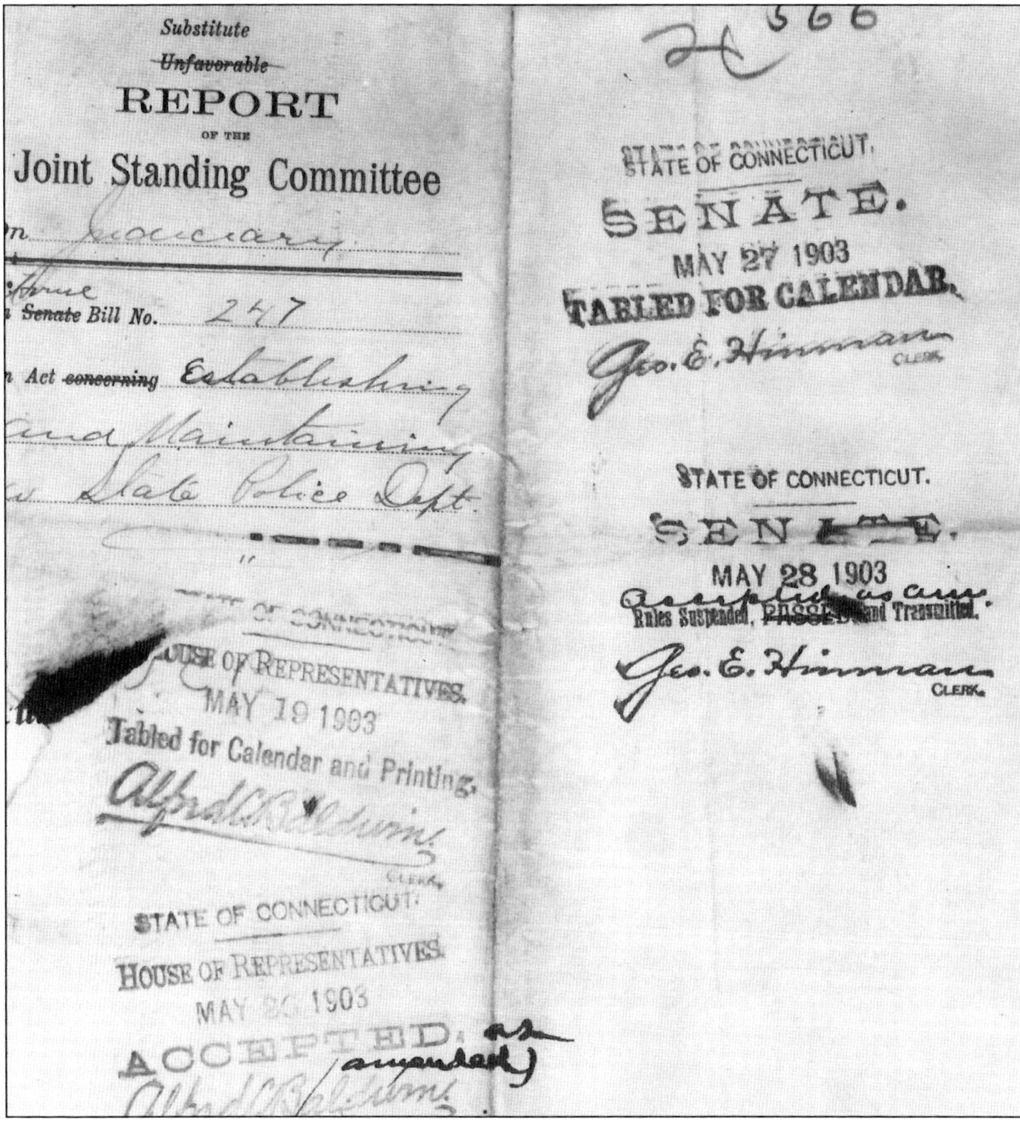
Substitute

~~Unfavorable~~

REPORT

OF THE

Joint Standing Committee

on Judiciary

House ~~Senate~~ Bill No. 247

An Act ~~concerning~~ Establishing and Maintaining a State Police Dept.

STATE OF CONNECTICUT

HOUSE OF REPRESENTATIVES

MAY 19 1903

Tabled for Calendar and Printing.

Alfred C. Baldwin

CLERK

STATE OF CONNECTICUT

HOUSE OF REPRESENTATIVES

MAY 26 1903

ACCEPTED as amended

Alfred C. Baldwin

566

STATE OF CONNECTICUT.

SENATE.

MAY 27 1903

TABLED FOR CALENDAR.

Geo. E. Hinman

CLERK

STATE OF CONNECTICUT.

SENATE.

MAY 28 1903

Accepted as am.

Rules Suspended, PASSED and Transmitted.

Geo. E. Hinman

CLERK

The substitute bill creating the Connecticut State Police Department is pictured here. Various committees through the hearing process marked it up before Gov. Abiram Chamberlain eventually affixed his signature in May 1903. Rep. Henry Goslee of Glastonbury sponsored House Bill 247 in January 1903. The Connecticut State Police Department was founded by this act of state legislature to combat crimes of vice, mainly liquor, gambling, and prostitution. One of the bill's authors was Samuel Thrasher, who also ran the temperance league and the Law and Order League, the precursor to the state police department. Thrasher was not named a prospective candidate to become this new department's leader. Just two years later, a bill attempted to abolish the department but failed. However, individual attempts to discredit the department's officers were made over the next decade or more.

The station in Danielson for Troop D is the backdrop for this dramatic photograph of two officers posing with their .32-caliber Colt revolvers. When officers were asked why they wanted to join the state police back then, the two most common replies were for the money and for the romance of it.

Pictured are state policemen from the western district barracks at a Hartford photography studio on Pearl Street. The state police had studios and photographers do most of their case and investigation photography until the 1920s, when several officers who possessed photography skills put darkrooms inside the barracks.

Considered a legend, Trooper Willard Bushy earned one of the highest ranks of the Connecticut State Police Department—lieutenant. He was a veteran of the Spanish-American War and World War I and was an avid collector of weapons. Bushy brought back, obtained, or purchased hundreds of war souvenirs. At the outbreak of World War II, he sold his precious collection to buy war bonds to support yet another war effort. The barracks and stations of the state police would contribute often to war bond drives, and Bushy was a major force behind these fundraisers. The barracks that contributed the most money to the war bond efforts received days off for its troopers. Trooper Bushy was a regular instructor at the academy and would become the department's first quartermaster.

Here, a trooper pumps water for his horse at his barracks. Horses were used often from 1903 until the 1920s, but none of them were actually owned by the state police. Many of these animals would be rented or leased by the day after the officer took the train or trolley to the area he needed to be working in. Officers were expected to carry enough money on their persons to use public transportation.

Troops are pictured here being inspected by Supt. Robert Hurley in the eastern district of the state. Hurley was appointed superintendent on July 21, 1921. He immediately swore in Trooper Alden McMurtry as a captain. Hurley swore in Thomas Egan, his old boss, as a deputy superintendent of weights and measures.

Supt. Robert Hurley was just an officer when he arrested horse thief Thomas Drapoe in 1908. Drapoe would eventually be held responsible for the thefts of at least 60 other horses. Hurley's experience in catching horse thieves was due in part to his being a horse trader and a detective in the late 1800s. During another chase of a horse thief, Hurley and State Policeman Jackson, who was an early member of the department, caused a man to fall from his stolen horse. Hurley said, "Jackson landed a haymaker on his jaw and knocked him out cold."

State of Connecticut
STATE POLICE DEPARTMENT
This is to Certify, That the Bearer
JOHN F. O'BRIEN
whose signature appears hereon, is a regularly appointed Officer of the Connecticut State Police Department, and as such is charged with the duty of investigating violations of the laws of the State of Connecticut, with authority to serve warrants and all criminal processes.

A Sunderland
COMMISSIONER STATE POLICE

John F. O'Brien
OFFICER

Officer John F. O'Brien was the bearer of this identification card. As the card reads, he was charged with the duties of investigating violations of laws of the State of Connecticut. This type of identification was unique for the late 1910s and early 1920s, as many law enforcement identifications at that time did not have photographs on them.

Pictured in the vicinity of Stafford Springs, Connecticut, are, from left to right, Bill Gruber, Ed Faeth, Frank Foley, Tom Leonard, and Joe Donovan. The Foley family would come to have three generations of troopers on the Connecticut State Police, and the most current member teaches at the Connecticut State Police Academy.

Officer Frank Baylis worked for four decades for the state police department and distinguished himself dozens of times. His personnel file is full of letters of commendation not only from his department but also from neighboring departments and states. Connecticut State Police Museum staff recovered his letters and uniforms at an antiques store in New Haven.

In the early part of the 1920s, the state police department suffered the loss of many officers at the hands of the motorcycle. This accident where a Connecticut State Police Department Henderson motorcycle struck a Chevrolet did not result in a fatality, but there were serious injuries.

Pictured in 1920 is the original Troop F. It was originally located in a house, and this grainy and torn photograph of a roll call or inspection was taken in the street because the building had no garage or space in the back. Very few pictures of this building exist today.

Connecticut license plate No. 167 is mounted on this Excelsior-Henderson motorcycle; this a crime scene photograph taken by Trooper Ernest Kirbell. Kirbell was a gifted photographer and was one of the first officers to take photographs of crime and accident scenes and develop them in the barracks.

Watching the neighborhood kids play on a hot summer day is all part of the patrol responsibilities for Officer John F. O'Brien. Most of the officers were known by the neighborhoods they patrolled, and many officers were placed on patrol close to their homes. The patrol technique, as seen in this photograph, occurred many years before the modern concept of community policing.

Two

The Roaring Twenties 1920–1929

Starting the in the 1920s, troopers were told to oversee amusement parks. Also, the tops of patrol cars were removed to help easily identify those of officers since all cars looked alike. Officers were using more photography, laundry markings, and wanted posters in their work and developing a keen sense of smell with regard to liquor violators.

In 1921, the department was reorganized, uniforms and badges were issued, motor vehicle examinations were given, and the first training academy opened. Before car radios, there was a night doorbell at the barracks, and citizens with phones would activate a red light or hoist a flag.

On Wednesday, November 15, 1922, Officer Pearle Roberts was the first state police officer to fall in the line of duty. He died in a motorcycle accident. In the mid-1920s, officers were attacking liquor, the Ku Klux Klan, and vice issues. In 1924, an employee named Zola Bennett passed away. Many years later, it was discovered that, though listed as a clerk, she was actually an investigator.

In 1925, three officers were terminated, while other officers were issued alcohol-testing equipment for use in the field. The following year, the department used an intercity teletype system, and sadly, in November 1926, Officer Bartholomew Skelly perished in a motorcycle accident.

Bulletins started to be issued regularly beginning in 1927, and one bulletin announced that practical jokes were banned. On July 20, 1927, Officers Paul Lavin and Harry Leavitt met Charles Lindbergh; they provided a motorcycle escort during his parade in Hartford. Also in 1927, the governor disbanded the state police commission and appointed a sole commissioner.

On April 6, 1928, Officer Irving Nelson was shot and killed chasing escaping felons. Three months later, Lloyd Eukers died in a motorcycle accident, and then Officer Stanley Hellberg, an eight-week trainee at the academy, fell from his motorcycle while practicing and died. These deaths caused a public outcry to ban the use of motorcycles. At the end of 1929, the state police had 100 cars and 100 motorcycles.

State police officer Pearle E. Roberts was the first officer in the state police department to be killed in the line of duty. His motorcycle tires got caught on trolley tracks, and he fell, hitting his head on a curbstone on November 15, 1922. He died of his injuries 10 days later on November 25. Roberts was a decorated veteran of World War I and left behind an expectant wife.

Charles Lindbergh (center) flew solo across the Atlantic Ocean in 1927 and became a national hero. On his return to the United States, he set out on a multicity tour, and one of his stops was Hartford, Connecticut. Lindbergh and his *Spirit of St. Louis* plane were protected and escorted by Lt. Paul Lavin (left) and Sgt. Harry Leavitt (right).

Several years ago, a man with a metal detector found an original state police badge No. 5 in a field. The number 5 is visible on collar ornaments and the badge of the unidentified officer in this photograph.

Trooper Kirbell snapped this 1927 photograph of a cruiser and motorcycles. They are parked at the converted carriage house of the Bulkeley Mansion, which had become headquarters to the state police. To the right of the carriage house is a brick garage, called the Lower Garage by troopers and civilians; it is still in use today.

On the left is Superintendent Hurley; he and state dignitaries are inspecting men and machines, seen at the rear, of 100 Washington Street in Hartford. To the far right is a sergeant wearing a sergeant major's rank, which most likely was his rank in the US military. This rank never existed within the state police department.

Trooper Paulsen investigates this accident at the request of Chief Grogan, head of the West Hartford Police Department. This cross cooperation was a common occurrence when there was a major crime or accident where complex tasks had to be performed.

This state police location was called Station No. 4. It would eventually become Troop C in Stafford Springs when it had its first full complement of men. To the extreme left is Sergeant Harmon; he became the first lieutenant in charge of Troop C. Harmon later resigned from the state police after striking a man in a fistfight who would later die of his injuries.

Here, two troopers show off both summer and winter wool gear. Wool jackets and long-sleeved shirts were worn year-round for decades regardless of the temperature. A member of the department in the 1940s remembered that the superintendent let the men unbutton their top button if the temperatures exceeded 100 degrees.

The family of former Connecticut governor Phineas Lounsbury leased this property in Ridgefield, Connecticut, to the state police department to be used as a barracks and academy. This c. 1925 photograph shows troopers and a small child, who most likely was a family member of a trooper in the photograph.

State police officer Carl E. Carlson is seen in his wool uniform, riding trousers, and puttees. The .32-caliber Colt revolver was standard, and Colt's manufacturing facility is only a mile from Connecticut State Police Department Headquarters. For many years, weapons were carried cross-draw style for protection; this was done because prisoners used to ride in the front seat next to the officer and could easily reach a weapon placed on the right side of the officer.

Here, state policemen investigate an airplane crash. Aircraft accidents began to steadily increase over the years, and so state troopers developed an expertise in looking into them. Accidents began to decline when severe safety measures combined with the accident reports created by law enforcement helped change airplanes' designs and operations.

This group of newly appointed sergeants is seen on the steps of the Hartford Supreme Courthouse. This building stands across the street from 100 Washington Street and is the current home of Troop H.

Plainclothes and uniformed officers investigate this crash, which not only caused injuries but also delayed the trolley from completing its run on time. Trolleys, though a good form of public transportation, were often responsible for accidents caused either by the trolley itself or the tracks.

This is a photograph of the front view of the Groton Barracks. This barracks moved and became Troop E in Montville, Connecticut. The new barracks is located off Interstate 384 and is also home to the major crime squad's large response van. The Groton Barracks' building is still intact.

These two officers are lined up for their patrol into eastern Connecticut. Pictured are, from left to right, Officer George Gardner, class of 1923, and Officer Henry Mayo, who joined the state police department the year this photograph was taken in 1929. Gardner eventually became the chief of the Killingly Police Department.

Academy uniforms would not become standard for many years. This class of smiling 1929 trooper trainees was being instructed on the grounds of the Ridgefield Academy and Barracks. Another thing that would not become standard until 1937 was the taking of a certified test to gain admission to the academy.

On the far right, Lt. Frederick Brandt has command over a group of officers. This location has a gas pump and may be a barracks or station. Troopers have a command structure somewhat like the military, and when a lieutenant was present, there were platoons of troopers overseen by sergeants and led by a lieutenant.

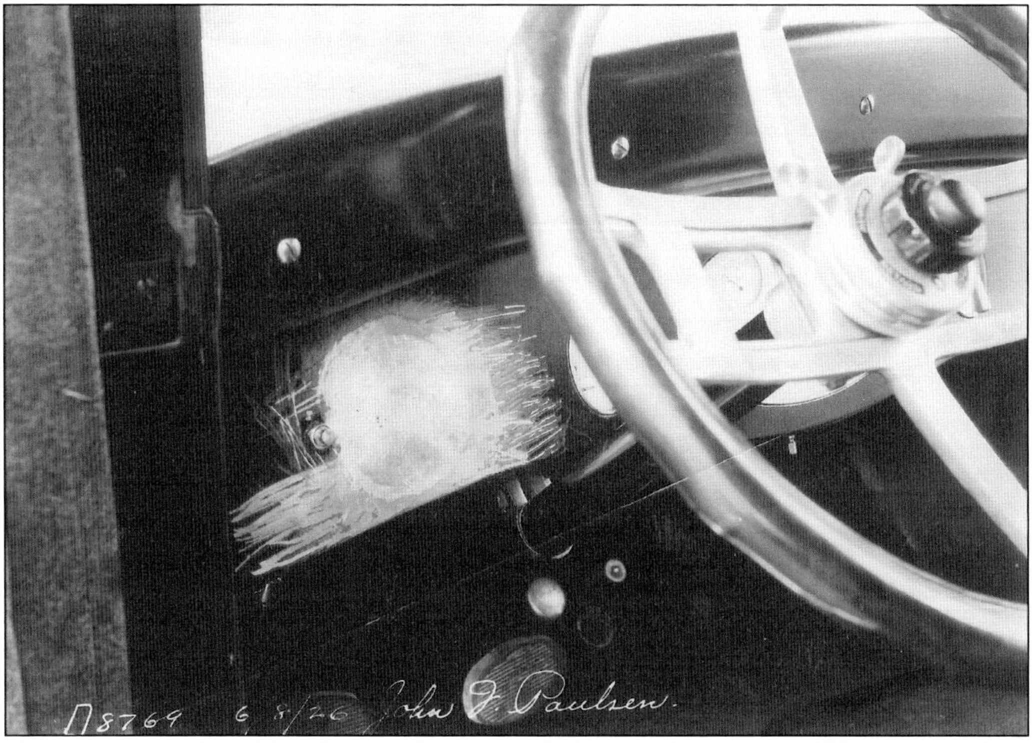

Many years after this 1920s photograph, motor vehicle manufacturers would begin to use long vehicle identification numbers. Prior to that security measure, they simply put a small and easily removed identification plate on the dashboard. In Troopers McKesson and Hansen's stolen-vehicle crime photograph, they show just how easy it was to remove the vehicle's plate and its identity.

Lt. Albert Field, who would eventually run the state police academy, shows off his technique of stopping vehicles through the use of one of the department's many Thompson submachine guns. The Thompson was issued to all barracks and stations, and there are still some survivors in the department's armory. One of them is on display at the state police museum in Meriden.

The ears of this vehicle's driver and the department's most senior member at the time, Sgt. Howard Williams, are being tested. Lt. Albert Field demonstrates firing a machine gun from a moving vehicle past the head of Williams. This technique was practiced along with small arms fire, and the training caused the department to purchase some vehicles with fold-down windshields to accommodate it.

After the order was given to remove the tops from all state police vehicles year-round, Sergeant Gardner took this photograph of his 1928-issued cruiser. This shows the amount of weather that the troopers were exposed to. To keep warm, many of the officers would bring kerosene lanterns and blankets. Some even took to stuffing newspapers insider their coats. The original complaint was that troopers were not visible to the public due to most vehicles appearing the same. There was an old saying that Henry Ford could make a car any color a customer wanted as long as it was black.

Here is Station D in on Route 12 in Danielson, Connecticut, in the late 1930s. Later, the troopers constructed a bricked barracks. The 1930s saw the expansion of barracks all across the state, and many of the barracks were of the same new design.

This cloudy photograph shows one of the rarest types of Henderson motorcycles; many today consider them collector's bikes. The motorcycles had large kerosene headlamps, which gave off dreadfully poor light, and troopers were in constant fear that they would blow out in the wind or from the bumpy road systems of the day.

Bantam, Connecticut, is the scene of this post-chase photograph of a rolled-over vehicle. At the conclusion of the chase, troopers made a common discovery—the truck was carrying illegal liquor products in its cargo. Arrests like these would continue and escalate during the 1920s and into the 1930s with the institution of Prohibition.

Trooper Porter Stannard, seen on his Henderson, may have been the first officer allowed the honor of getting married in his uniform. His son allowed the author the privilege of seeing his wedding photographs taken at the Ridgefield Station, which had beautiful grounds and wraparound porches. The bride does not wear white but has on a print dress in that photograph.

Three

The Great Depression 1929–1939

During Prohibition, the state police officers were busy catching those illegally selling and buying alcohol. One time, while walking from headquarters in Hartford, a state police officer even spied men unloading liquor into a building across the street. At this time, the use of weapons on duty was increasing, and many troopers had registered machine guns. Though shot at from the running boards of a cruiser, one of Officer Nelson's killers escaped, but he was captured in Florida after having killed an officer there. Huge caches of liquor, vehicles, and vessels were seized at a routine rate, and there was one time when a yacht was seized with over $50,000 worth of liquor on board.

Also in the 1930s, Commissioner Anthony Sunderland created an aerial division through a lend-or-lease program with aircraft owned by large companies. Though a new division was started, in 1931, there were only 10 positions for new hires in the state police department, and over 3,000 applicants applied for them. In October 1932, Leonard Watson was killed in a motorcycle accident while on duty at the Yale versus Army football game in New Haven. The department's loaned aircraft in 1933 were used often to locate stills and cockfighting arenas. More than 40 stills were located and more than 5,000 arrests were made with the help of these loaned aircraft. At this time also, officers licensed motor vehicle races. In 1934, the first canines were trained and used by the state police.

The Bureau of Identification started in the 1930s, and it still maintains all criminal photographs and fingerprints today. Sunderland purchased 50 Indian Motorcycles for $373 apiece and 16 Studebakers with fold-down windshields so that supervisors could shoot while they drove.

Applicants in 1937–1938 had to be between 23 and 30 years old, between five feet, nine inches and six feet tall, and 155 to 200 pounds.

The year 1938 saw a steep increase in narcotics and trafficking while the 1938 hurricane devastated Connecticut, causing hundreds of deaths. State police assisted every town with loss of life and victim recovery. And toward end the decade, in 1939, a two-way radio system for police cars was installed and an alcohol-testing device was created for drivers.

Seen here, a rumrunner's car and moonshine are taken by the police. The moonshine was being transported in milk cans. Every possible way one could think of to transport liquor was used during this time period. When applicants to the state police were tested in those days, along with a regular physical, they had to have a good sense of smell. Being able to smell alcohol was critical in uncovering smuggled liquor.

Nineteen troopers line up under the command of the lieutenant on the far left, Frederick Brandt. The lieutenant would head up public relations later in his career and act as a department spokesman. This lineup was for an unknown event.

Trooper Carlton Klocker was good at identifying disguised liquor in trucks and cars. In this October 1932 stop, the moonshine was hidden behind large wooden spools. The demand for illegal liquor during Prohibition made every vehicle moving a potential target for troopers on patrol. One technique was for troopers to watch the purchase of goods such as sugar in markets to get clues to the locations of stills.

With every accident, there is a lot of paperwork the troopers have to fill out. Running from the police is never a good idea, and this bootlegger learned that the hard way in this 1931 crash. A lot of accidents occurred during chases due to the poor mechanical and speed capabilities of automobiles and trucks of the period.

The grand opening of Groton Barracks in 1932 had all hands and equipment on deck, as seen here. The barracks would close years later, and its substitute, Troop E, opened in Montville. Troop E currently serves a large area of towns that have no organized police departments and a large piece of Interstate 95.

Trooper Wallace Nelson directs traffic and investigates this early-1933 fatal accident. At the time of this photograph, Nelson had been on the state police for many years already yet was still wearing the wool blouse that bore the football-shaped patch with state police on it. This may have been a first-issue uniform for him; all troopers were only issued one.

Lt. Michael Smith, the plainclothes officer in the center of this picture, represented the state police department in shooting competitions for many years. Sporting the classic 1930s shooting method of the day with one hand on his hip and one eye closed, Officer Harry Ritchie is on the far right.

Troopers participate in most parades and have for at least 100 years. They are asked to participate in all the standard holiday rituals, inaugurations, and funerals of department members. Pictured in this 1930s photograph, Trooper Albert Pethick is on the right. Due to Connecticut being one of the original 13 colonies, the state police color guard participates in presidential inaugurations too.

One of the reasons the weights and measures division was established was to prevent the cheating of consumers. Some foods commanded a dear price during the Depression, and unscrupulous people often took advantage of customers. This case in 1934 stopped a gang from making and selling counterfeit oleomargarine medicine. The gang would mix hazardous chemicals in unsanitary conditions to produce the fake, and sometimes dangerous, medicine.

A family member of Trooper Frank Baylis, pictured on the far right, sold his collection of photographs and other items to an antique store in New Haven, Connecticut, where the author purchased them. In this 1933 photograph, this group of five practices shooting craft in a pit. There was no range for many years, and sandpits and extremely rural locations became makeshift ranges.

Here is a better view of the crude shooting pit that Trooper Baylis, seen on the far right, and his peers are practicing at. It appears to have been carved out of the ground by construction equipment. Troopers were allotted ammunition to practice with, and anything over that allotment came out of the officer's pocket.

Many police departments in the state had Harley-Davidson motorcycles, and most people in Connecticut believe, as do many past and present police officers, that they were the standard choice of the Connecticut state police. That was not the case with the Connecticut State Police, and this photograph from 1936 is the first known to show Harley-Davidsons operated by Connecticut troopers.

Troopers from an emergency services unit and patrol gather at the scene of a downed commercial aircraft in the western part of Connecticut. The president of Eastern Airlines wrote the state police to thank them for their handling of this investigation. The president of the airline was World War I ace, Medal of Honor recipient, and Indy 500–winner Eddie Rickenbacker.

Commissioner Hickey (front row, left) stands with newly appointed sergeants at the headquarters building on Washington Street in Hartford. This building still stands but is being utilized by other state agencies. Troop H in Hartford is located directly behind this structure and department headquarters is now located in Middletown, Connecticut.

Trooper Edward Engstram had an adventure on the high seas that the state police historians still speak of today. In 1935, when it came to his attention that a boat was illegally harvesting oysters, Engstram commandeered a boat. He approached and identified himself, and the boat captain took off, causing a seven-hour chase. It all ended when Engstram shot the captain in the leg.

As the war in Europe began to escalate, officers in Connecticut were beginning to prepare for eventual US involvement. These two officers are working in an emergency communications office, and the officer on the right is using a telegraph. That old form of technology could be put into action quickly if phone lines were severed. Pictured on the left is Officer Charlie Pritchard.

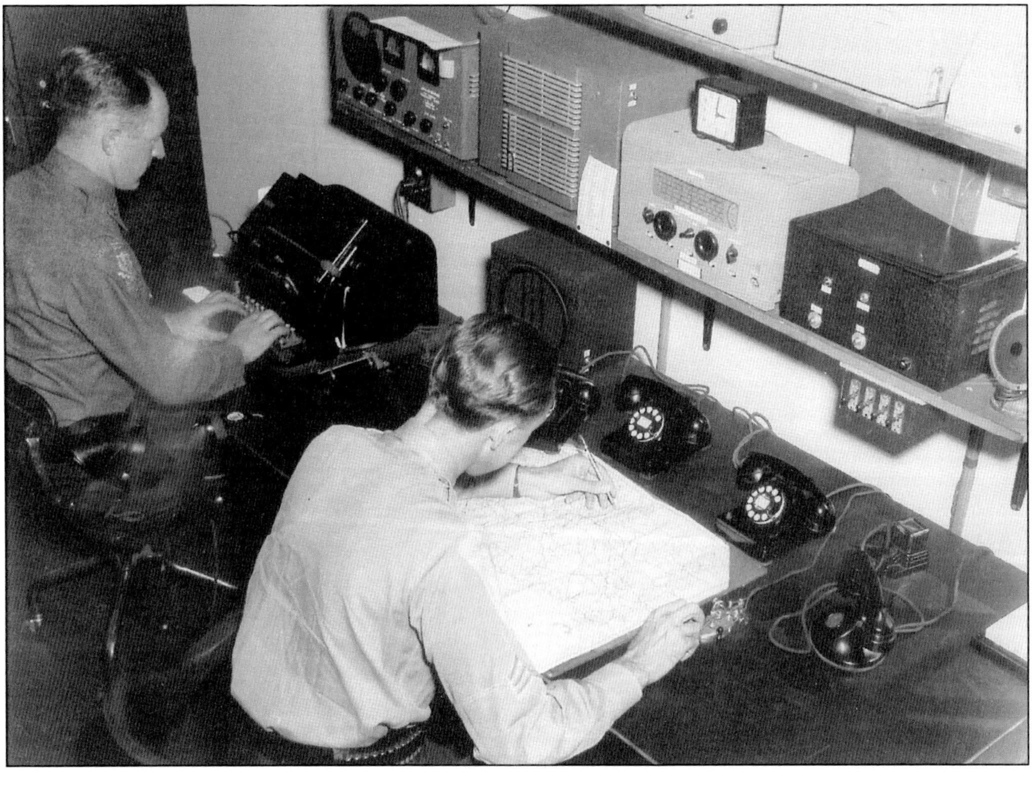

This 1938 photograph shows the replacement structure for the Bulkeley Mansion, which had been headquarters at 100 Washington Street. Bulkeley Mansion was demolished and was replaced by this limestone building, which would remain a headquarters of the state police for many decades.

In 1935, J. Edgar Hoover began a program, which is still in effect today, called the National Academy. Hand-selected supervisors and administrators from law enforcement agencies all over the country attend academy classes given by the Federal Bureau of Investigation (FBI) year-round in Quantico, Virginia. Future commissioner Leo J. Mulcahy received this autograph of Hoover after graduating from the very first class in 1935.

A demonstration of state police equipment at an unidentified exposition highlights the weights and measures division. The only responsibility of the weights and measures division still within the purview of the state police is that regarding overweight trucks. That responsibility is split with the inspectors division of the motor vehicle department.

This 1937 truck was built especially for the weights and measures division of the state police to check and regulate the sale of gasoline. The vehicle cost $2,000 and was operated by Trooper Carlton Klocker. It would have gallons of gas pumped from a business into a tank, and there was a measuring device to insure that the public was not cheated at the pumps.

This large gathering of the state police on their motorcycles took place in Bridgeport, Connecticut, in 1938; the reason for the grouping is unknown. One of the possibilities for such a large gather would have been a strike or a submarine launching. Many times and due to its popularity in those days, the Yale football games drew huge crowds that needed help from the state police.

Under the watchful eye of a federal agent in the background, these troopers are practicing with the Thompson submachine gun. The weapon in the hands of underworld figures did tremendous damage to both good and bad for many years. The .45-caliber round is devastating, but the weapon undoubtedly saved lives while in the hands of law enforcement.

Lt. Harris Hulburt (left) and Commissioner Edward Hickey (right) stand in front of a contingent of officers at Station C. This barracks was built in farmhouse style with large boards and stonework. The building was a favorite police barracks for several generations of troopers. It is currently a senior center and still has operational prison cells.

Chef Capron serves up another meal to the troopers at a barracks. As part of their compensation, officers could eat their meals at the barracks. This also served them well as they would often pull weeklong duties at a time. When an officer was assigned kitchen duty, it was said that he was working in the "*China Clipper*," whose meaning is lost to history.

On March 9, 1932, Trooper Lionel Poirier climbed into the back of a truck loaded with sugar. He knew it was making deliveries to illegal stills. The truck made stops for hours, and at the last stop, he leapt from the truck and arrested six men at the site with a gun in each hand. He later became known as "Two Guns" for that arrest effort. This recovery of $50,000 worth of equipment and material was not his only outstanding memory. A year later, he would stop Amelia Earhart for speeding, and she would autograph a dollar bill for him, which the family kept for generations and has since donated to the Connecticut State Police Museum. She had, according to reports from the family and the media of the day, argued with Trooper Poirier that drivers should have medical certificates like pilots and maintain them.

Lionel "Two Guns" Poirier (second from right) stands for a photograph with the still he seized along with other officials. The still pictured here produced thousands of gallons of illegal liquor each year and serviced several towns and dozens of small liquor sales establishments. Records showed that given the time period, the profits were described as staggering.

Prior to the invention of metal guardrails, safety barriers, and signs, wooden fences, signs, and barriers were shattered on impact, causing devastating effects for both the car and driver, as this 1930 photograph taken by Trooper Kirbell indicates. Many of today's improved highway systems and equipment were born from accident statistics and investigations.

The still featured in this photograph is on a farm. Farms were a great place to hide the types of equipment needed to operate a still. They had large plots of land, running water, privacy, and outbuildings.

New to the state police department in 1937 was an emergency services unit truck. This truck was a 1937 Brockway, which sported a six-cylinder flathead engine and could carry tons of equipment to on- and off-road locations.

Members of the state police recruit class of 1937 were called the Blue Ribbon Boys. That was due to the fact that they were the first class to enter the academy after having taken a state-certified entrance examination. This class would have its members teased for years because of their test taking. Many times over the years, different state agencies would administer these types of tests, and the results would vary.

William A. Gruber carried one of the first weapons purchased and issued to the department by Colt's manufacturing facility in Hartford. It is known that the weapon, with the stamp "CSP No. 19," was turned over to the state police archives. Colt confirmed this weapon was in a batch of 20 made especially for the department.

Four

THE IMPACT OF WAR
THE 1940S

On May 1, 1940, the first two-way modulated radio system developed by Fred Link and Dr. Daniel E. Noble, also a pioneer at Motorola, was tested. The year 1941 also saw J. Edgar Hoover open a National Academy office in Connecticut to deal with spies, and the Auxiliary State Police program was implemented to support troopers. Two state policewomen, Kathryn Haggerty and Evelyn Briggs, were appointed in 1941; they were sent to the NYPD for training because it was set up to train women. Though gaining two officers, the department lost one, Sgt. Charles Hill. He was struck by two vehicles at a stop. Also, 44 state police and 38 civilian members of the department joined the war effort, and Commissioner Hickey headed the defense council.

In 1942, ten Germans were arrested for spying. They had binoculars, maps, revolvers, rifles, and 11 shortwave radios. Speedboats were placed into action in June 1943. Officer Jesmonth would strike a tree and lose his life while driving to an emergency in July 1943. While patrolling the waterways of the state, Lt. Kenneth Stevens spilled into the water and died after the boat ran into a submerged object in June 1944.

Also in the 1940s, the Resident State Trooper program was implemented in Pine Meadow. When the war ended, one of the best assignments that the state police officers could have was driving servicemen and women home from the train and bus stations.

Checking vehicles with calibrated equipment was new for the state police in 1947. When the Automatic Signal Company of Norwalk, Connecticut, first tested the Electro-matic Speed Meter, it only had a range of 150 feet.

Air and sea rescues were practiced off the coast of Connecticut. In 1948, the Civil Defense System picked Commissioner Hickey as only one of 11 individuals to contribute to its board. In February 1948, the radar device, having been tested, allowed Officers Kimball and Gedney to make the first radar arrest in Glastonbury. Lt. Frank Starkel was struck and killed by a rock at a construction site while overseeing its blasting on July 19, 1948.

This photograph of a tired but prepared commissioner is dated December 8, 1941. The day after Japan attacked the United States, Commissioner Hickey and the state police department were fully prepared to deal with the war. Hickey was in charge of the war department for the state, and he had already begun hiring provisional officers to replace those going off to war. He also oversaw and ordered first-aid training for all personnel and appointed auxiliaries who would check bridges and infrastructure. All defense plant security personnel would come under his jurisdiction and were sworn in as special state police. When the war was in full swing, the officers, both men and women, would escort explosives, troops, and other assets across the state. Spies would be hunted, and the department was responsible for hundreds of deportations of undesirable citizens.

The 1940 graduates are seen here with their pith helmets, which became standard headgear for the department, lasting past the end of World War II. The graduates made $95 per month and would work, eat, and sleep out of a barracks for seven-day-long periods, 24 hours a day. With their graduation completed, they brought the department up to approximately 225 officers. Pictured are, from left to right, (first row) Major Frank Nichols, Henry Wilcoxson, John Faughnan, Robert O'Grady, Joseph Bodie and Commissioner Edward Hickey; (second row) George Boston, Joseph Glynn, Charles Kiernan, and Edward Steele; (third row) Robert Brown, Thomas Smith, Henry Kaliss, and Joe Lastauskas; (fourth row) Robert Murphy, Walter Perkins, Ed Formeister, and Henry Marikle; (fifth row) Marcel Simon, Robert Abel, James Dick, and Robert Bohman.

Featured in this c. 1940 photograph are, from left to right, Sgt. Charles Hill, Officer Edwin Pequignot, Sgt. George Remer, and Officers Casey and Foley. Sergeant Hill wearing a straw hat, which the department wore for only a two-year period, would fall in the line of duty in 1941.

A headquarters inspection in the early 1940s is visible in this dark photograph. Constant inspection was something that the state police commissioner would insist upon. A state of readiness that knew no equal in Connecticut law enforcement existed due in large part to the war and the department's tremendous responsibilities.

Members of the emergency service crew in this May 1940 photograph are, from left to right, Officers Spencer, Schwartz, and Curran. These officers received specialized training in first aid, rescue, downed aircraft, and water and cave rescues, amongst many other things. The truck's equipment inventory changed constantly to best help the task at hand, but sometimes, policy would dictate a change in the equipment.

A weights and measures station is featured. Troopers would search for equipment violations and overweight trucks. An overweight truck is often responsible for smuggling, roadway damage, and/or accidents. The current fines for overweight trucks, unlike in the decade of this photograph, can run into the tens of thousands of dollars.

Commissioner Hickey requested, and was granted by an act of the Connecticut General Assembly, that he be allowed to appoint two women to the department as state policewomen. This occurred on March 11, 1941, for Kathryn Haggerty (left) and Evelyn Briggs. Commissioner Valentine accepted the women into the New York City Police Department Academy with express permission. They attended the New York City academy because it had the facilities to train women police candidates. They trained for six weeks and were assigned at first to protect the morals and behavior of women and children. Their roles expanded, as did their investigative responsibilities, as their careers progressed. They were paid more than their male counterparts due to their having a college degree/nursing certificate as a requirement. Although there are several photographs of these two women in uniform, they rarely wore them while working.

Here is a briefing about rationing during the war; it was held at headquarters and was put on by the commissioner's staff. Enforcement of food coupon books and gasoline were the main concerns. Seated in the center of this large briefing are the two original state policewomen, Briggs (right) and Haggerty.

Troopers learn how to maintain their motorcycles in this 1941 academy class photograph. Every trooper had to complete a lengthy inspection sheet of all issued equipment, which was checked carefully by a supervisor. That practice continues today, and the inspection sheets now contain everything from issued uniforms to weapons.

Trooper Reardon checks out the height of the snow in the town of Goshen, Connecticut. A senior citizen at a speech given by a trooper in Litchfield, Connecticut, went up to the officer afterwards and parted with this photograph. She had held onto it for approximately 50 years.

Roll call at Station D in Danielson in 1940 includes, from left to right, Officers Mackenzie, Powell, Poirier, Gowdy, Delaney, Konopaska, and Reardon and Sergeant Lavery. The photograph reads, "41," but the plate on the car has the year 1940. License plates in Connecticut for many decades were issued every year.

Trooper Otto Haffersat rides a department Indian on patrol through eastern Connecticut. The motorcycles of the state police were purchased over the years more for their cost than their efficiency. The state police switched from Henderson motorcycles to Indian to Harley to Kawasaki and back again to Harley over many decades.

Airplane disaster training is being conducted in this photograph taken at the Bridgeport Airfield. Much training like this was common in anticipation of US involvement with the war in Europe. Airplane identification charts were issued to all barracks and special state police to assist in the location and direction of potential enemy aircraft.

Two bloodhounds and their handlers appear to be on an apparent track or training mission. The canine program in the Connecticut State Police Department gained a worldwide reputation, and many of the handlers and trainers have been loaned to other departments and, in some cases, other countries to assist in training.

Safety and civil defense with regard to the state's highways and the war effort caused these types of vehicles to be designed to broadcast messages or warnings to the state's citizens. Various signs were available at the barracks and in specialty vehicles and could be put into any situation quickly.

Many state police cruisers during the war years carried large signage with various messages available. This is an accident scene with a large reflective warning sign. Poor lighting in vehicles was one reason the signs were so large.

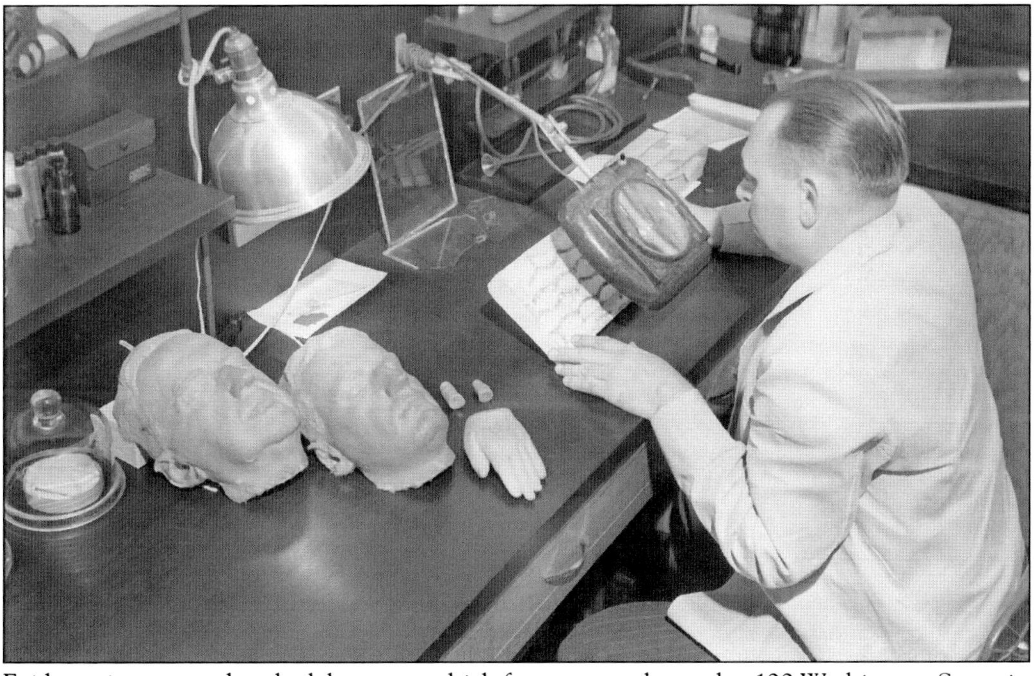

Evidence is processed at the laboratory, which for years was located at 100 Washington Street in the headquarters building. Molds of the human face, also called death masks, along with limbs were used to make identifications. The forensic laboratories were not united in their disciplines, and many times a single trooper would be the only expert in a particular field.

This wartime photograph shows a critical responsibility of the state police, which was the protected movements of weapons, explosives, men, and other supplies across the state. Huge transport responsibilities were heaped on the state police department, and many of them were carried out under the cover of darkness to prevent detection by the enemy.

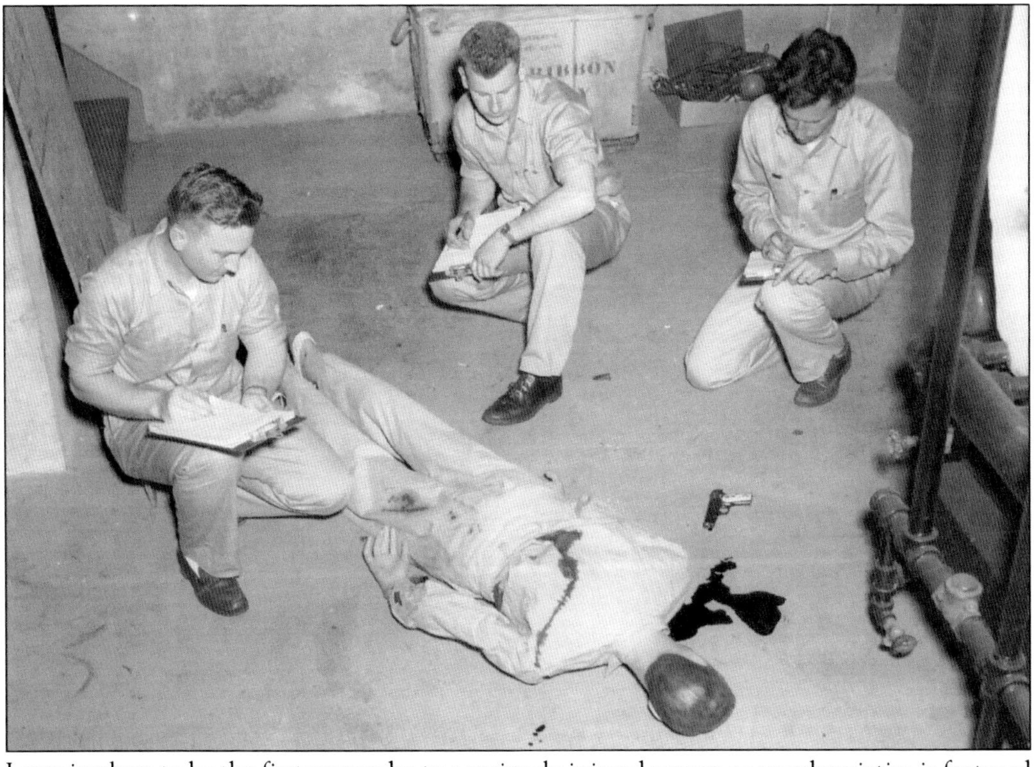

Learning how to be the first responder to a seriously injured person or murder victim is featured in this academy training session from the 1940s. First-aid training is a standard course in all academies, and there are yearly updates and in-service training for troopers.

Troop A Barracks is pictured in 1943; these men are still wearing breeches and puttees while the officer in the middle wears regular slacks and shoes. Overlaps of uniform styles were common. The rationing of clothing materials, certain metals, and leather caused the repurposing of everything.

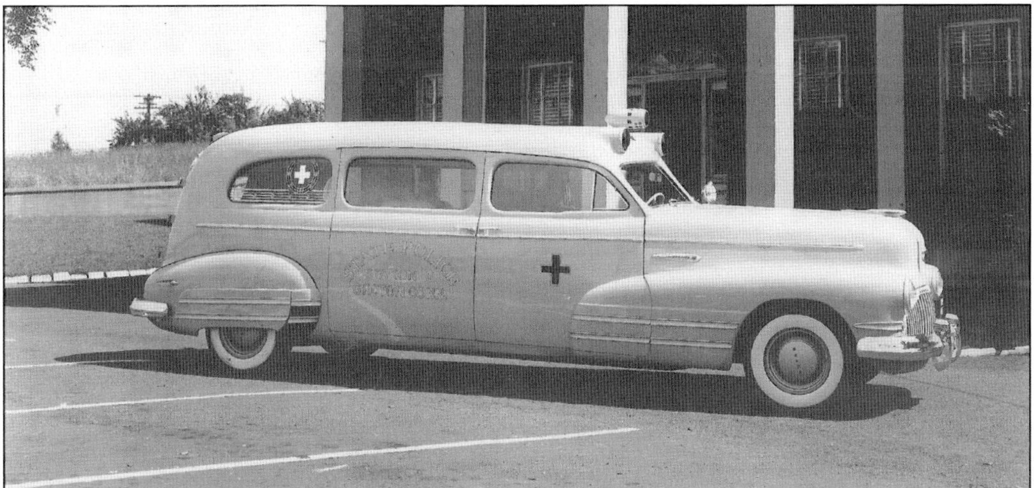

After implementing plans across the state to deal with the potential for mass casualties, most barracks became equipped with ambulances. They were used mainly for motor vehicle accidents. This 1942 ambulance, shown in 1944, was typical, and most of them were donated. In the 1940s, any trooper who was close by during a tragedy would operate the ambulance.

The 1947 Danbury Fair detail includes, from left to right, Troopers Larry Beizer, Ken Tripp, Joe Ciezierski, Leon Merritt, Bill McNamara, Edward McMahon, and Sal Esposito. In front is the spokesman for the Phillip Morris Cigarette Company, Johnny Roventini.

These men are gathered for Sgt. Les Williams's promotion to lieutenant in 1948. Pictured are, from left to right, Bill Gruber, Les Williams, Lou Marchese, Larry Beizer, and Terry Zemetis. Williams would go on to teach at the academy for many years and wrote a lot of the teaching materials and training guides used at the academy.

On July 6, 1944, the Ringling Bros. and Barnum & Bailey Circus was performing in Hartford. A fire broke out in a tent and grounds, crowded with nearly 6,000 people. When it was over, there were 168 killed and more than 500 injured. In the crowd that day, with several family members, was state police commissioner Hickey. As the state's fire marshal and an administrator of the war council, he oversaw the setting up of a large morgue in the Armory Building, located a mile away. One of the causes of the fire was the use of flammable materials to waterproof the tent. One little girl went unidentified for many decades, and firemen would place flowers on her grave every year. She was known as Little Miss 1565, for her grave identification number. She was identified 47 years after the fire as Eleanor Cook, age eight.

It is not just another day at the beach in the summer of 1948 when a large shark washes up on shore and causes a scene. Many of the shore town communities in 1948 were under the authority of the state police department, which still patrols approximately half of the towns in Connecticut.

Touring the submarine base in New London is Pres. Franklin D. Roosevelt (left). The Secret Service and Trooper Reardon, with the Pith helmet, escort him. To Roosevelt's right is an ecstatic Commissioner Hickey of the state police. This base was one of the most important and guarded sites in America during World War II.

Pictured is the 1949 inauguration of Gov. Chester Bowles; troopers are seen marching in the rain. They are passing under a landmark called the Memorial Arch close to the capitol. The state police would escort the governor for events, and current governors have a detail of state police assigned to them 24 hours a day.

Keeping the waterways safe during the war was the main reason this river patrol boat was created. It carried machine guns both fore and aft. The state police department showed this craft off during a parade in July 1942. These machine guns, though impressive, were never used in anger during the war.

The 1941 Mercury was the vehicle chosen for installation of one of the country's first two-way radio systems. It would be copied by both the military and the Secret Service soon after Prof. Dan Noble and radio designer Fred Link developed it. The Army Tank Corps used the technology to allow tanks to communicate without huge antennas.

Giving a summons to a motorist on Interstate 91 in front of the Colt manufacturing facility around 1949 is Trooper Roy Paige. The blue dome of the Colt building is one of the most recognizable structures in the United States.

Five

A Country on the Move
The 1950s

During the 1950s, hundreds of drive-in theaters sprang up, and the movies inspectors' arm of the department was tested. A wire photograph system that could transmit a picture, prints, or single-page documents was put into place, and in 1951, it was connected to three locations—Boston, New York City, and the FBI in Virginia. On June 9, 1951, a bank was robbed in Woodbury, Connecticut. This crime led to a manhunt that lasted for days and ended in a shoot-out with state police. The bank had been used previously for a movie location about a bank robbery.

Governor Lodge appointed Edward Hickey head of the civil defense department. The troopers began registering laundry mats and laundry marks. The crime lab began using death mask impressions in wax for later identification. Hundreds of arrests and thousands of crime photographs were processed, and even the department ambulances were busy. Those ambulances were transporting approximately 500 patients a year.

On February 13, 1953, Trooper Ernest Morse stopped a young man for speeding. The young man shot Trooper Morse and left him on the side of the road, where several Good Samaritans found him and helped him pray the rosary before he died.

The Resident State Trooper program expanded rapidly, and department members took approximately 17,000 complaints per year in the 1950s. Cornell University compiled motor vehicle and accident statistics, and Connecticut provided many of those statistics to help improve vehicle safety. Lieutenant Steele called headquarters on August 19, 1955, to report a river had overrun its banks; this was at the beginning of the Flood of 1955. Two officers nearly drowned when their cars were swept away. Hundreds were rescued by helicopters.

Auxiliary officer Donald Evans invented the Fingerprint Comparator. The device increased the view of a fingerprint by 20 times; it cost $150. Arthur Colombe and Joseph "Mad Dog" Taborsky killed seven people in just a few weeks, and Taborsky wound up on death row for the second time. Commissioner Mulcahy reorganized the department once again by creating large specialized units.

Here, Commissioner Hickey goes for a ride on a state police Harley-Davidson with a sidecar. The sidecars were purchased during the war for the purpose of having a second officer who could shoot or transport important messages or materials. Every piece of equipment under Hickey's regime often had multiple purposes.

Getting a flat tire in the late 1940s was a big deal due to severe rubber shortages and rationing of tires because of the war efforts.

Pres. Harry Truman (backseat, left) is escorted through the military contractors' buildings in the state; one escort is Trooper Pethick. Trooper Pethick has the white hat and is on the far side at the passenger door of the limousine. Many presidents would visit the state because of its strategic importance and its contributions to the previous war efforts and anticipated ones.

Troopers, many of them veterans of World Wars I and II, are present for the 1950 dedication of the Blue Star Memorial Highway. This system was dedicated for veterans of World War II.

Connecticut's first two state policewomen and other law enforcement officials are pictured here attending a 1950 seminar on homicide investigation at Harvard. Seated on the near left side of the table are, from left to right, state policewomen Haggerty and Briggs. After their initial hiring, the women took on more expanded duties and roles within the department.

Sgt. Vernon Gedney runs the radar box in 1951 in the Hartford area. He and Trooper Albert Kimball wrote the first ticket issued by radar in the United States in the town of Glastonbury several years earlier in 1947. Kimball, when interviewed prior to his death, could not recall which one of the two of them had actually written the first ticket but was able to certify it was one of them.

Det. Samuel Rome (right), who would rise to the rank of major, elicits a confession from the suspect, in the center with arms extended. A victim was later recovered at this riverside location in 1950. Rome, who lived in Hartford, was well known as a friend to the children in his neighborhood.

Troopers and their small wooden boats are seen working hard to rescue people from a flood in Rowayton, Connecticut, in the spring of 1950. Floods are always something the department prepares and trains for.

In the early 1950s, there was a large expansion of the state police auxiliary as well as state trooper marine patrols on the state's waterways. This group is made up almost exclusively of state police auxiliaries. The auxiliary would often work weekends, and this supplement to the regular state police force was crucial to the department's success.

As a convenience to motorists, and if a driver were willing to plead guilty in 1951 by the roadside, he could post his bond or pay his ticket at this portable station. The options now are quite different, of course, and this method would not be appreciated in modern society.

President Eisenhower is escorted through the streets of East Hartford, Connecticut, in 1952. Part of his escort included Commissioner Leo Mulcahy at the left rear of the vehicle in sunglasses and Maj. Samuel Rome at the right rear of the president's vehicle. They are passing the now-defunct East Hartford Hospital, as is evident by the nursing staff members close by.

Vehicle inspections were essential to being prepared for anything. This early-1950s photograph not only shows the basic equipment spread out but also the massive Link radio system in the trunk. Trunk and under-the-hood inspections were quite common.

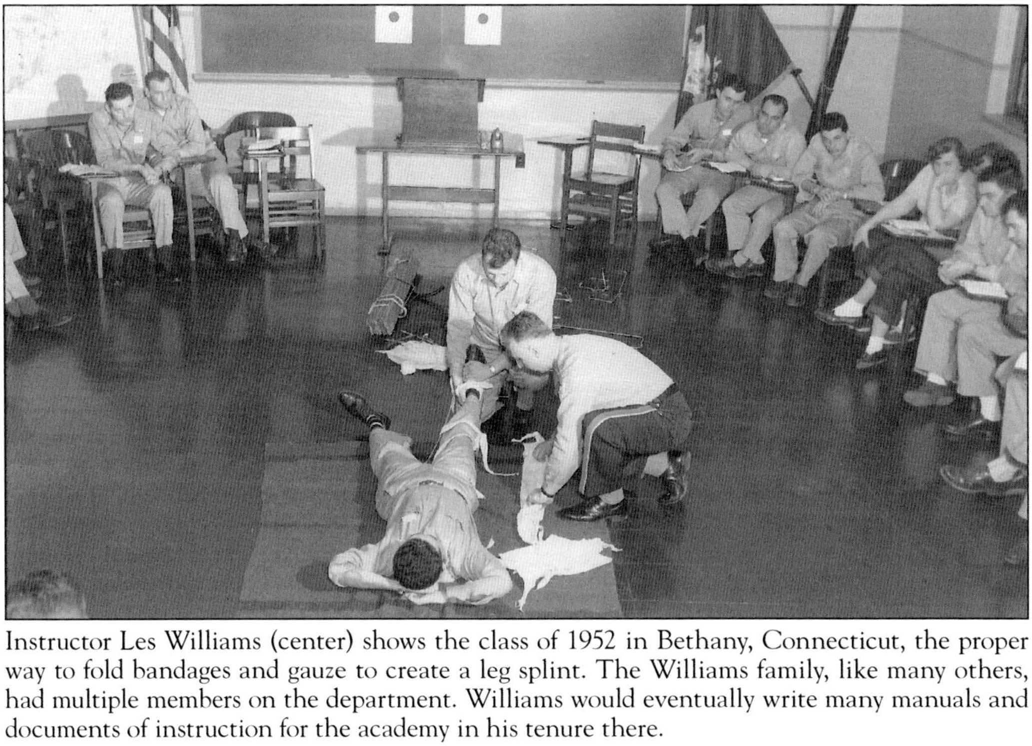

Instructor Les Williams (center) shows the class of 1952 in Bethany, Connecticut, the proper way to fold bandages and gauze to create a leg splint. The Williams family, like many others, had multiple members on the department. Williams would eventually write many manuals and documents of instruction for the academy in his tenure there.

Troopers and aviation investigators search for answers in this loss-of-life crash in the woods of western Connecticut around 1953. During World War II and continuing past the Korean War, troopers received a lot of training in aircraft accident and learned to treat injuries caused by them.

This photograph shows a close-up of a trooper with a seat from the plane crash. It is a somber reminder to the officer that someone was sitting in that seat most likely just hours before the incident. In the current administration, counselors for mass tragedies are available for officers. Counseling was most certainly not available for approximately the first 70 years of the department's existence.

The passing of Commissioner Edward Hickey, who had served the Connecticut State Police on and off from 1922 until his death in 1953, brought thousands of mourners to his funeral. His efforts as the man in charge of the military and state police departments during the war were recognized worldwide.

State police detectives using strings are recording the path of a bullet, which took the life of a liquor store clerk in the early 1950s. This type of evidence collection is crucial to the successful conviction of criminals, and though still used, it is often done now with lasers.

George Boston runs radar on a bridge overlooking the Merritt Parkway. Chase cars wait below. Boston's car had to remain in place due to all the equipment being attached to it.

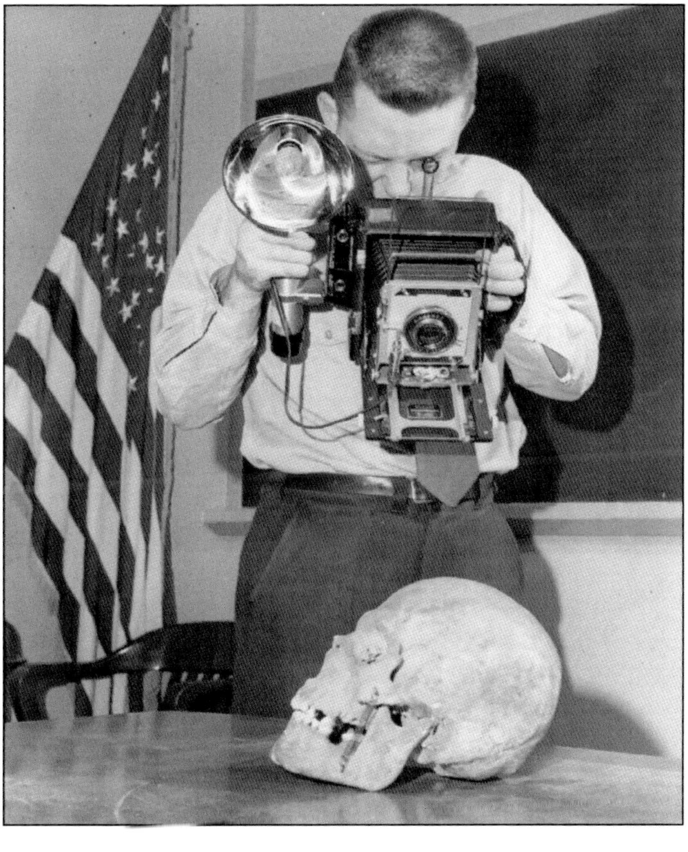

Academy trainee Ray Reynolds hones his photography skills using an old press camera to take a picture of a human skull in this 1956 classroom. Photography skills are important for a good investigation, and after evidence is destroyed by man or nature, the photograph is a permanent record of what was there during the crime or incident.

Wearing both long and short winter coats, two troopers investigate a 1955 accident and fire, which had a sad ending.

Marked light-blue station wagons were used as parkway cars; many were driven by auxiliaries, as the station wagons had large payloads. These 1950s cars were also given the affectionate pet name of "Blue Goose." Oftentimes, a speed clock was mounted to inform motorists how fast they were traveling.

Escorted by the state police, President Eisenhower (center, carrying hat) and Gov. Abraham Ribicoff (talking with Eisenhower), examine the damage to the *Connecticut* caused by the 1955 flood. Sgt. Edward Steele made the first call about the flood. He advised headquarters that the Farmington River had just overflowed its banks. While inspecting the damage, the governor and his driver Sergeant Horan's car suddenly filled up with water, the governor hitched a ride back to Hartford in a milk truck. Several other cruisers were washed away, and one officer was nearly killed. Helicopters were pressed into service from Sikorsky, Kaman, Pratt & Whitney, and the Connecticut Air Guard. Many officers did not see home for days and were put up at citizens' homes or businesses.

Insurance company advertisements featuring the state police were common in the 1950s. Trooper Louis Stefanek, who served from the mid-1940s until the mid-1970s, is seen in this ad, which touted, "Drive like they are in the car with you." The state also had billboards with safety slogans and once had a contest for the catchiest saying.

This cherished photograph was taken in 1954 at the home of the commissioner's secretary, Rose Albright. Lt. Edward C. Steele, who was then a sergeant, places the wreath on the door around the holidays. Lieutenant Steele assisted the author on this project, and at the time of its writing, he was 100 years old.

Trooper Williams demonstrates one of the first sets of seat belts installed into cruisers in 1955. Many cars did not come with seat belts; rather, they were an option. Children used to sit in the backseat unbelted or stand up in the rear seat while the vehicle was being operated.

Trainee Edward Pickett (in the back row on the left) watches one of his classmates in 1959 get slammed to the mat in judo class. Various forms of martial arts are taught at the training academies. In the 1950s, judo was most prevalent. Pickett would not spend a long time in uniform and would find a job as an inspector the state's attorney's office.

State police classes are identified not only by the year of entry but also by a session or training troop number. This 1954 class was the 51st training troop. The length of training classes has changed many times over the years; currently, state police trainees spend approximately 28 weeks in the academy.

Edward Pickett Sr. shows off new cell doors inside a barracks in the late 1950s. Trooper Pickett was assigned to the new Troop F Barracks from the academy. At the time of this book's creation, Troop F is installing a walkway of brick engraved with the names of troopers who served at that site over the years.

Idling just downriver from the Portland Bridge in Middletown, Connecticut, is this late-1950s 19-foot-long river patrol boat. The operator is Dr. Stanley M. Lund, an optometrist and state police auxiliary. Dr. Lund was not only an auxiliary, but he was also a state police surgeon.

A 1952 parade in Monroe, Connecticut, shows off state police equipment from both the past and present. A parade is always a test of how well a group can march together, which is a good indicator of training and discipline. Parades are also a source of pride for a department.

Trooper Walter Stecko leads an honor guard at a parade on the grounds of the US Coast Guard Academy in New London. Trooper Stecko eventually achieved the rank of lieutenant colonel.

The dispatcher at any barracks or troop is a valuable entity. These two troopers are dispatching cars for numerous towns and hundreds of miles of highway from Troop H in Hartford. During a rain or snowstorm, a barracks can see an influx of telephone calls from the public, which can range from dozens of calls to hundreds.

Six

Civil Unrest and Technology

The 1960s

Previously serving as a radar officer on a World War II bomber, Trooper Nelson Hurlburt was a radar expert for the department in the 1960s. Troopers John Doyle and Robert Riemer were the first operators of the Stoelting polygraph machine. The auxiliary program in 1963 was expanded to the water with donated patrol boats.

On October 29, 1960, a drunk driver hit 24-year-old Trooper James A Lambert at a call; Lambert had been a trooper only seven months when he passed away. In 1964, Albert Washington was the first black male to attend an academy class; he was a former Navy diver.

On August 6, 1962, Joseph Stoba went to a domestic call in Portland. Stanley Czaja, who had a history of disorderly behavior, shot Stoba in the chest, killing him. Troopers started analyzing voiceprints for cases on the Spectrograph. Clip-on ties were ordered to prevent strangulation during a struggle, and Cruiser taillights were rewired so they flashed when stopped.

The living quarters of trooper trainees were on a Navy barge; they were nicknamed the floating class. They would eventually earn $89.66 per week.

Connecticut officers interviewed a rapist in Massachusetts, and he confessed to crimes in Connecticut. Further investigation showed that Albert DeSalvo was wanted in the Boston area as the Boston Strangler.

In 1966, duties of monitoring bingo and a shadow program, which allowed troopers to see what belonging to different units would be like, were started. Unrest led to rioting in most of Connecticut's cities, and troopers were assigned to every location to supplement the forces there.

Cruisers in the 1960s were equipped with video cameras, and mace issued was declared a hazardous material. The late 1960s saw advances, as Louise Smith became the first black state policewoman. Doris Hughes was promoted to detective and went on to become the first female lieutenant in the department.

Black Panther member Alex Rackley was killed and dumped in a swamp. This case would tie up the state police for two years. Defendants would become known as the New Haven Nine. Their trial in 1970 set a record for cost.

The troopers and auxiliaries held a record hop for 300 teenagers in 1960 at Troop F. Coordinating the efforts are, from left to right, Lt. Vernon Gedney, auxiliary Lynn Selby, and Trooper Robert Dee. Standing just inside the bus is Trooper Douglas Patterson. This type of community outreach is important work and breeds cooperation and respect from the public.

Here is an Independence Day parade in 1962 with the state police auxiliary color guard leading the way. Auxiliaries include, from left to right, Burdick, Taft, Togg, and Littell. An auxiliary also takes great pride in representing the department and his or her branch of it. The pride is evident, as many of the auxiliaries are giving up time with their families to perform valuable functions for free.

This is an early-1960s guide written for the academy staff by the lieutenant on how he wants a recruit's equipment to be laid out on his or her bunk. The current administration and operations manual is hundreds of pages long and is available on a disk. It covers everything from haircuts to fire extinguisher maintenance.

Trooper Rinkalib, seen in the background, investigates this fatal accident. In an attached report from 1963, the notation of bald tires, along with speed, was made a contributing factor to the accident. Finding the reason for an accident is the reason the state police do accident investigations. The victim in an accident deserves an answer, and the offender need to be cited for any wrongdoing. An investigation establishes cause, which often dictates the way cases are handled in either civil or criminal courts.

President Kennedy (center) is flanked to his left by Governor Ribicoff and plainclothes state police detectives on his 1961 visit to the state capitol. The Kennedy family had close ties to Connecticut, and many family members lived in the state. A lot of family members also went to Yale University in New Haven.

All troopers appreciate their cars and the mechanics who maintain them. This 1963 birthday party at Troop G is for its mechanic George Gereg, seen front and center. The mechanics got the troopers going and kept them going.

Christmas and holiday parties have always been celebrated with great enthusiasm at the barracks and stations. This party was held at the state police range in Simsbury in the winter of 1965. Troops and their families often enjoy holiday parties, Easter egg hunts, and themed events.

Accident investigation is a day-to-day occurrence for troopers in Connecticut. Figuring out what happened is sometimes done using math or hard work. The trooper at this Berlin, Connecticut, accident from 1964 seems to be using a little of both by piecing together the parts of the car.

The same 1964 Berlin, Connecticut, accident scene included several pieces of information that helped solve this hit-and-run accident. Glass, paint chips, and pieces of chrome left behind can put a motor vehicle offender at the scene of a crime or an accident.

Troopers and civilians are shown accepting a book on uniform traffic laws. The motor vehicle laws being made uniform in the early 1960s made the training and enforcing the same on the state and local levels. Constant changes in the laws cause troopers in the field to pay close attention to the latest information or revision.

This is an eastern district traffic squad briefing from April 1961. Pictured, from left to right, are Furman "Soupy" Campbell, John Tucker, Robert "Red" Heatherman, Sgt. Frank Dowling, Ronald Luneau, and Roger Boske. Briefings of all kinds are important to get everyone involved on the same page, increasing safety and efficiency.

In the early 1960s, a marked station wagon with a speed clock on its roof was destroyed in this accident. There were no serious injuries, but the auxiliary officer driving it had a lot of paperwork to fill out. Department accidents are or could be investigated by not only the state police department but also by any local department with jurisdiction.

This ladies' club meeting in the 1960s was highlighted by a bloodhound demonstration put on by auxiliary trooper Armand Rossanelli. K-9 demonstrations are one of the most popular things the state police do in a public venue. They always get rave reviews from kids and adults and are especially effective in schools.

Radar sets for traffic enforcement are slowly being squeezed out by lasers, but back in 1965, Trooper Tim Murphy had what was then the latest technology, and it was referred to as the box. Some of these units were pretty messy to use, as the speed would be recorded in red ink. The ink stains on the carpets of a cruiser are a telltale sign that an officer wrote a lot of tickets.

This is a 1960s celebration for which Governor Dempsey was in attendance. Most graduations, promotion ceremonies, and larger retirement parties send out invitations to seated and retired governors. The state police have a governor security detail around the clock, and its members also travel with the governor. The coverage for the head of state is 24 hours a day.

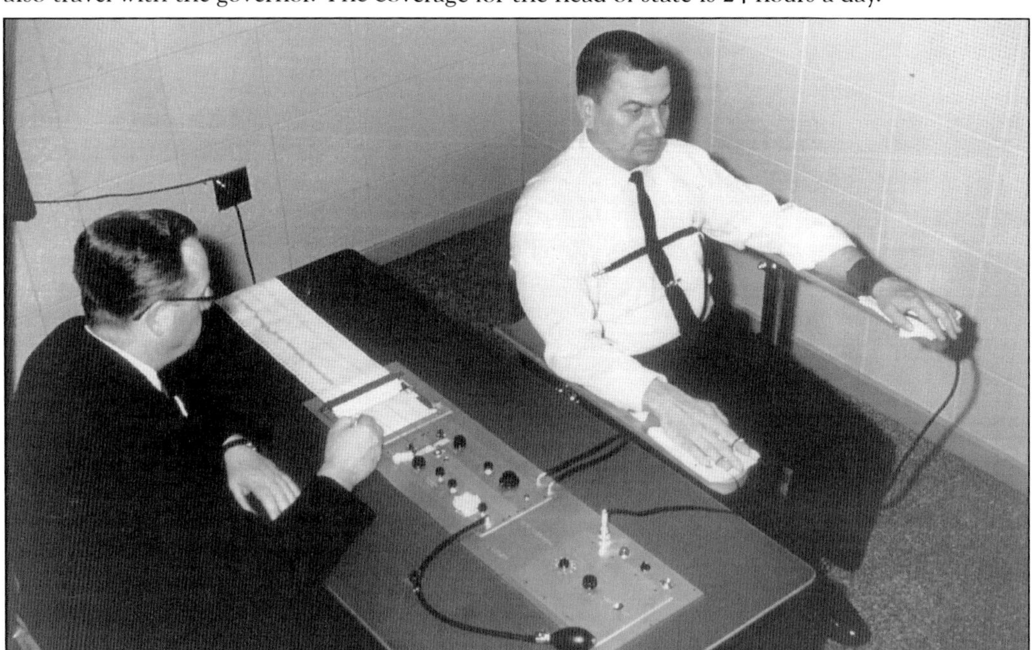

Headquarters designated a special room for the polygraph machine in the early 1960s. The first machine cost approximately $1,500. Its first trained operators were Sgt. John Doyle and Trooper Robert Riemer. Because of its vacuum tubes, it took around 30 minutes to warm up.

Air Force copilot James Ellis explains to Trooper Alfred Hull that the Boeing Vertol 21 Helicopter developed engine failure over the interstate. Pilot H.W. Trail and his crew spent several hours dismantling the blades so that the helicopter could be towed away. According to a report attached to the photograph, the Air Force was not issued a summons for this incident.

Here, troopers in Hartford handle this 1963 accident on Interstate 91 after the operator of the station wagon stopped to look at his map in the high-speed lane. The Volkswagen operator perished due to the other driver's lapse in judgment. Seat belts may not have saved this person, but the use of them was becoming a hot topic for safety in the early 1960s.

Riots in the large cities during the turbulent 1960s often saw the state police role as one of supplementing the city police departments. Troopers Hurley (left) and McDonald wear standard-issue riot helmets and safety glasses. Troopers would be assigned to neighborhoods with the city officers who knew the areas well.

This paddy wagon in New Haven is being filled with rioters or looters as state troopers and New Haven police officers work together to restore order. Looting and other crimes would spiral out of control, and the National Guard would supplement the city and state police on occasion.

As protests spilled onto the campuses, this 1968 winter event was on the campus of the University of Connecticut. Students, teachers, and outside protestors alike were cited after things got out of hand on the campus. The state policewomen present took female protestors into custody.

Trooper Angelo Buffa types a report from his notes. The manual typewriter, carbon paper, and erasers were the only report writing technology available prior to the digital age. Spell-checking was done by an officer's supervisor, not a computer. Mistakes were underlined or circled in red pen or pencil and had to be retyped.

Trooper Bill Shaw escorts Nike missiles through Connecticut in 1963.

Trooper Walter Stecko lays a wreath at a memorial service for all of the Connecticut troopers killed in the line of duty between 1903 and the date of this photograph in 1966. Unfortunately, that number has risen since 1966 by quite a few. In Meriden, Connecticut, there is a memorial to all officers who have fallen, and the names go back to the 1800s.

Performing traffic duty is something every police officer has to do at some point in his or her career. Officers here are directing people into an event at the fairgrounds in Danbury, Connecticut.

Traffic enforcement to reduce accidents is featured in this mid-1960s photograph. The device on the roof of the station wagon is a speed clock, which showed approaching vehicles how fast they were traveling. Smaller digital devices are used now, and many of them are even solar powered.

Troopers at a staged roadblock close in for the arrest with guns drawn. This photograph is of an officer safety program that was being developed in the late 1960s. A lot of promotional videos, pamphlets, and posters exist in which troopers are displayed.

Trooper Edward Brymer and his canine partner Blitz are shown in this 1968 photograph. Trooper Brymer would later become the deputy chief of the East Hartford Police Department and then would become the chief of the Middletown Police Department. Many troopers in the past and present have taken on the role of chief in local departments.

Between the Cold War and the increased flow of nuclear items being transported on the interstates, most departments, like the state police in this 1965 photograph, began extensive training with Geiger counters. The disaster training and the distribution of disaster materials were taken very seriously for many years. Home bunkers and fallout shelters were everywhere.

While practicing at the range in 1966, Trooper William Ellert's fired shot was captured on film. The bullet can be seen leaving a trail as it heads down range to the target. Weapons training is of course one of the most important things taught and maintained in any department. The job of carrying a gun for a living has an awesome responsibility attached to it.

This is a large-scale search for a missing man in June 1965. The search parties include volunteer firemen and Sgt. Rocky Brozek (left) and Trooper Joe Ciercierski (right). Search and rescue is a common occurrence, and the technology changes have been critical to recent successes with the addition of such things as infrared devices and helicopters.

Seen working on their military drill skills in May 1960 are state police auxiliaries. Hundreds of auxiliaries have donated hundreds of thousands of man-hour's dong things that allow troopers to focus their efforts elsewhere. Some of these duties range from transporting blood to standing behind accident scenes; their contributions are incalculable.

Seven

More Technology
The 1970s and Early 1980s

In the 1970s, driver's licenses finally came online at the motor vehicle department, red lights on cruiser roof racks were switched to blue, and .38-caliber pistols were replaced with .357 Magnums. Internal affairs and wiretapping units were created at this time, while the height requirement for troopers was done away with.

The 1970s state police department saw an increase in speed when it purchased Plymouth Furys. A government-surplus Huey helicopter was acquired by the state police and was pressed into service in 1976. The first pilots were Troopers Bastedo and Maguder, both Vietnam veterans. One Friday the 13th in 1976, Trooper Carl Moller and a motorist were struck and killed.

The statewide narcotics task force was born, and 56 window-mounted radar sets were added to patrol cars. In 1978, a truck enforcement squad was created; there were three teams of five men. At the governor's request, 1978 saw the creation of a pursuit policy.

A serial-killer task force was created to deal with the deaths of at least five women. The rigging of games at jai alai was overseen by a one-man grand jury. A national fuel crisis affected the state police, which ordered all cruisers to be switched off for 15 minutes every hour.

On October 3, 1979, a tornado ripped through the Windsor Locks area. Several people were killed, and plans implemented by the state police went into effect. Troopers were also sent to New Hampshire to deal with nuclear plant protestors.

In 1980, an arson task force was created. Governor Grasso signed a bill that maintained widows' benefits for troopers killed in the line of duty. The Connecticut Supreme Court deemed state police bloodhound Clem qualified and highly trained to do his job.

An Intoximeter 3000, which tests breath samples, was installed at all state police barracks.

On December 6, 1982, Lt. Thomas F. Carney died when a truck driver deliberately tried to pass close enough to blow his hat off but struck him instead. Lastly, motorcycles returned to the department when four Kawasaki KZ-1000P models were purchased.

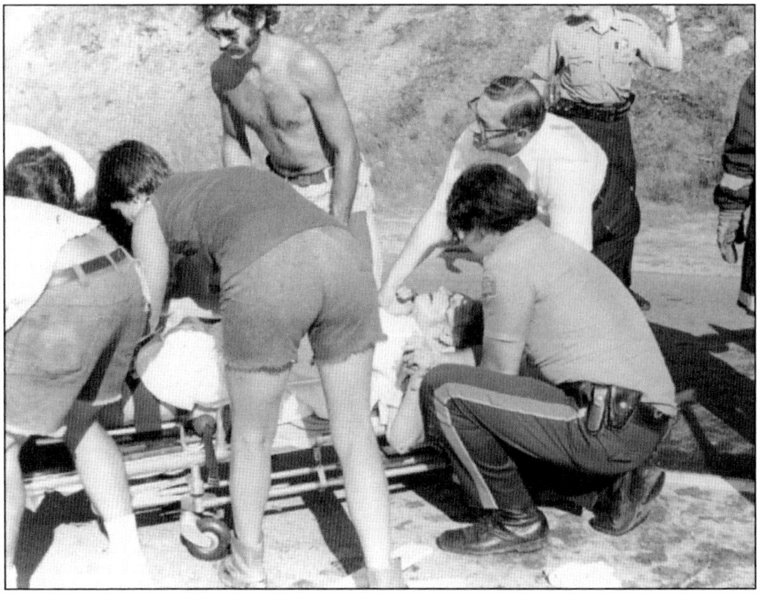

Holding the hand of a scared citizen who had the misfortune to crash his car in 1970, this trooper exemplifies the first rule of arriving at a scene. That rule is to secure the scene and help the injured. Troopers have to be aware of a lot of things at scenes like these. Those things range from hazardous conditions to a hand that needs to held.

The State Police Dive Team spends time with a youth group in this 1972 photograph. Divers pictured, from left to right, are Ken Barton, George Hamilla, Jimmy Minor, and Ron Bergin. All state police divers are Navy certified and are cross-trained in various disciplines. Barton devotes much of his time to the alumni association, museum, and newsletter, which he authors.

Commissioner Leo J. Mulcahy, pictured here as a captain, worked for the state police department from 1930 until 1971. He rose through the ranks and had an accomplished career. In 1935, he attended the National Academy of the FBI, the first of its kind. There, he became friends with J. Edgar Hoover. Mulcahy became an academy instructor and, in 1955, was appointed by Governor Ribicoff to head the Civil Defense Agency of Connecticut. In 1959, he began his 12-year run as the state police commissioner. Also in 1959, he officially changed the names of department officers to troopers. On July 12, 1982, the 32-acre state police complex in Meriden was renamed the Leo J. Mulcahy Complex.

Photograph processing in the barracks was an important aspect of police work. Here, Det. Dan Hurley is setting a negative up to be enlarged around 1970. The photograph processing business is dying, and the digital age is taking over. Note that enlarged photographs developed in lab conditions like this were very crisp and extremely detailed.

Gov. Thomas J. Meskill speaks with state troopers at the Eastern States Exposition in 1974. The exposition site has buildings designed specifically for each New England state, and the interior relates to that state. Even though the fairgrounds is located in Massachusetts, when inside the Connecticut building, the Connecticut troopers have jurisdiction.

The troopers responding to this 1975 bank robbery in Montville, Connecticut, are discussing tactics. In the foreground are, from left to right, Troopers Avery, Leitkowski, and Nurse. Though many bank robberies shift to the FBI, the first responder and the information gathered right away solve most cases like these.

This arrest by undercover and heavily armed state police officers occurred in 1975; no more information is known about the action taking place in this photograph.

The city of Stratford fire personnel along with the state police and fire marshal's office conducted this 1979 training class. The participants were learning about vehicle arson. Many fire and police departments will tear a car apart or burn one to improve their skill sets and, quite often at the same time, increase public awareness.

World-renowned forensic scientist and former state police commissioner Dr. Henry C. Lee holds an outdoor arson class.

The canine unit is in charge of obtaining and training new specialty canines. This training was used to create the world's first accelerant detection dog. Mattie the Labrador became the nation's first arson detection dog. Her success led to the training of other specialty animals for narcotics, explosives, and body recoveries.

In this late-1970s photograph, Connecticut and New Hampshire state police get together for motorcycle training and techniques in New Hampshire. Trooper Bob Kenney is in the center of this group. He went on to have a long career working to identify outlaw motorcycle gangs. He also developed expertise in the recovery of stolen motorcycles and motorcycle parts.

Seen at 100 Washington Street in Hartford is the class of 1970. This 76th Training Troop would be the last to train at the Bethany Barracks. Many graduates of the academy take great pride in being the first or last class to train at a facility. One class was on a Navy barge while several were run at a monastery.

The class of 1982, which would graduate in May 1983, is seen here at graduation in the auditorium of Central Connecticut State University. It would be the largest class so far to graduate. The 92nd Training Troop was taught for 28 weeks at a temporary academy set up to handle its size in the Mystic Oral School in Mystic, Connecticut.

Whenever trouble spills over at a correctional facility, the state police, seen here in 1977 at a maximum-security prison in Somers, are called in to supplement the guards. The prison systems in Connecticut, however, now have specialized units and teams highly trained to quell most situations.

Few are chosen to become specialized accident investigators, but all are required to develop great skills at mapmaking, sketching, and reasoning when trying to determine the cause of an accident. In this 1982 crash in Tolland, Connecticut, the trooper is doing just that. The math portions of an accident reconstruction class are intense, and the graduates of those specialty classes are always in high demand.

Taken in front of the state and municipal police academy is this image of a trooper with his c. 1974 Plymouth Fury. The Fury was very fast, and the department used this car for only a brief time in the mid-1970s. Parts of the exhaust system on the Fury would get so hot that, if the trooper were parked on the grass, it sometimes would catch on fire.

To this day, slot machines are illegal in Connecticut to possess or operate outside of a casino. Here, Lieutenant Hurley inspects the slot and pull-tab machines from a 1970 vice raid. In an agreement with Indian tribes in Connecticut, Gov. Lowell Weicker would allow slot machines in the state, but only on designated reservations.

Diving into deep and cold waters is always extremely hazardous, and this Navy-certified state police diver found himself in some distress in this 1983 incident. Diving in many of the state's quarries is quite dangerous because they often contain vehicles and other debris.

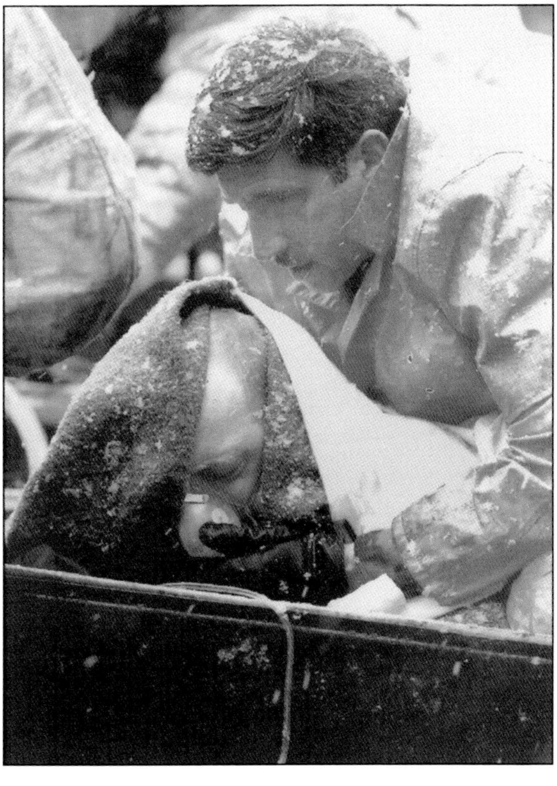

This tractor-trailer accident in a snowstorm created a special problem for first responders as the driver became entangled in the wreckage. Under these miserable conditions, Trooper Theodore Wojtusik, covered in snow, provides reassurance and oxygen to the injured while rescue workers are hard at work to free this victim.

This closed-door briefing for a narcotics raid in 1975 resulted in the execution of search or arrest warrants and drug seizures. Raids like these can take lots of planning, which is critical to their outcome. To get the desired effect, all involved must be on the same page, and safety is stressed.

In the late 1970s, the New England states took on a program called CARE. This stood for Combined Accident Reduction Effort. Grant monies were spent to increase traffic squads and radar patrols on the highways in the east to reduce injuries. Pictured in Connecticut state police uniforms are, from left to right, Trooper Michael Finnegan and Trooper Louis Heller.

The ever-vigilant Trooper Don Grover patrols his town. Though this photograph is from the late 1950s, the tradition remains the same. All troopers take an oath on their graduation, and a part of it reads, "I am a soldier of the law, to me is entrusted the honor of the department."

This uniform was first worn in 1983. The uniform with the newly designed shirts, patches, and pants, which included the addition of a Beretta 92 with a 15-round magazine, soon won national recognition for the department when officers were chosen as the best dressed in their category.

The patch from Lt. Thomas F. Carney's jacket is clearly visible in the side of this trailer. The tractor-trailer combination struck Lieutenant Carney as he was assisting a motorist. He was killed on Interstate 84 on December 6, 1982, when a truck driver deliberately tried to pass close enough to blow his hat off but struck him instead. The term *dusting* was used as a joke on law enforcement officers when truckers would do this. This tragedy was absolutely preventable—unlike so many others. Lt. Carney's patch is a symbol for all the recruits at the academy of the hazards, honor, and sacrifices made in serving others.

About the Connecticut State Police Alumni Association

The Connecticut State Police Alumni Association was founded in 1972. It has several component parts. The fraternal organization requires that a member graduate from the state police academy. The Educational Foundation collects and distributes scholarships to the children of the men and women of the state police department. The last component is the museum, which houses the photographs, recordings, equipment, and history of the department. The author's proceeds from this work are all earmarked for the museum project.

These organizational component parts all work together to promote the department and the welfare of its members, both sworn and civilian. Their goal is to keep the membership healthy and informed. The motto of all three sections is the same—Never Forget.

This work covers the images of a department from 1903 until approximately 1983. Since then, the Connecticut state police have found themselves on the edge of history many times. The men and women of the state police have run toward and not from the rubble at Ground Zero in New York City after both September 11th and the tragedy involving the shootings of small children in Newtown, Connecticut, at the Sandy Hook Elementary School. The members of the Connecticut State Police Department listed below all adhered to the following oath to the end of their watch and into the department's history books:

> I am a Connecticut State Trooper, a soldier of the law. To me is entrusted the honor of the department. I will serve the State of Connecticut honestly and faithfully and if need be, lay down my life as others have done rather than swerve from the path of duty. I will be loyal to my superiors, obey the law and enforce the law without discrimination as to class, color, creed, or condition, and without fear or favor. I will help those in danger or distress, and at all times conduct myself so as to uphold the honor of the department.

The department's fallen members are listed below.

Trooper Pearle E. Roberts, 11/25/22
Trooper Bartholomew M. Skelly, 11/11/25
Trooper Irving H. Nelson, 4/06/28
Trooper Lloyd J. Eukers, 7/21/28
Trooper Stanley H. Hellberg, 6/01/29
Trooper Leonard H. Watson, 10/22/32
Sgt. Charles F. Hill, 11/06/41
Trooper Edward P. Jesmonth, 7/20/43
Lt. Kenneth W. Stevens, 6/06/44
Lt. Frank A. Starkel, 7/19/48
Trooper Ernest J. Morse, 2/13/53
Trooper James W. Lambert, 10/29/60
Trooper Joseph M. Stoba Jr., 8/06/62
Trooper Carl P. Moller, 2/13/76;
Lt. Thomas F. Carney, 10/12/82
Trooper James Savage, 1/22/86
Trooper Jorge Agosto, 11/22/89
Trooper Russell Bagshaw, 6/05/91
Aux. Trooper Edward Truelove, 11/13/92
Aux. Trooper Phillip A. Mingione, 5/25/94
Trooper FC Kenneth R. Hall, 9/02/10